100 facts
Extreme Earth

100 facts

Extreme Earth

Anna Claybourne

Consultant: Camilla de la Bedoyere

First published as hardback in 2008 by Miles Kelly Publishing Ltd
Bardfield Centre, Great Bardfield, Essex, CM7 4SL, UK

This edition published 2010

2 4 6 8 10 9 7 5 3 1

Editorial Director: Belinda Gallagher
Art Director: Jo Brewer
Editorial Assistant: Sarah Parkin
Volume Designer: Simon Lee
Indexer: Gill Lee
Production Manager: Elizabeth Brunwin
Reprographics: Anthony Cambray, Ian Paulyn
Editions Manager: Bethan Ellish

ISBN 978-1-84810-232-3

Printed in China

British Library Cataloguing-in-Publication Data
A catalogue record for this book is available from the British Library

ACKNOWLEDGEMENTS
The publishers would like to thank the following artists who have contributed to this book:
Richard Burgess, Mike Foster
All other artworks from the Miles Kelly Artwork Bank

The publishers would like to thank the following sources for the use of their photographs:
Cover photograph: Roza/Fotolia
Page 6 Gary Braasch/Corbis; 8(l) Topham Picturepoint/TopFoto.co.uk, (r) QiangBa DanZhen/Fotolia.com;
11 Yann Arthus-Bertrand/Corbis; 12 David Samuel Robbins/Corbis; 14 Steve Vidler/Photolibrary;
15(l) Albo/Fotolia.com, (r) Pablo Corral V/Corbis; 16(t) JTB Photo/Photolibrary, (b) NASA;
18(t) Robert Dowling/Corbis, (b) Stephen Alvarez/Getty Images; 19 Javier Trueba/MSF/Science Photo Library;
20 Phil Degginger/Photolibrary; 21(t) JTB Photo/Photolibrary, (b) Paul Chesley/Getty Images;
22 Jeremy Horner/Corbis; 23(l) NASA, (r) NASA; 25(b) Frans Lemmens/Zefa/Corbis;
26(t) Tim Davis/Corbis, (b) Rick Price/Corbis; 29(t) Paul A. Souders/Corbis, (b) Colin Monteath/Photolibrary;
32 Image Source/Corbis; 35(l) Nick Hawkes/Ecoscene, (r) Peter Menzel/Science Photo Library;
36(t) Jim Reed/FLPA, (b) Denis Balibouse/Reuters; 37 AFP/Getty Images;
38(t) flucas@Fotolia.com, (m) Aurora/Getty Images; 39 Reuters/Corbis; 40 Eric Nguyen/Corbis;
42 Warren Faidley/Corbis; 44(t) NASA, (b) Mike Goldwater/Getty Images; 45(t) Sipa Press/Rexfeatures;
46 C A.Ishokon-UNEP/Still Pictures; 47(b) NOAA/Science Photo Library
All other photographs are from:
Corel, digitalSTOCK, digitalvision, iStockphoto.com, John Foxx,
PhotoAlto, PhotoDisc, PhotoEssentials, PhotoPro, Stockbyte

Made with paper from a sustainable forest

www.mileskelly.net
info@mileskelly.net

www.factsforprojects.com
The one-stop homework helper — pictures, facts, videos, projects and more

Contents

Our extreme Earth

▶ A wave crashes ashore on rocks at Cape Arago, Oregon, USA, throwing up a huge fountain of spray. Heavy waves can sink boats, smash buildings and sweep people off the shore.

1 The Earth is a planet of extremes. At the North and South Poles, freezing temperatures reach as low as –40°C. Meanwhile, hot water gushes out from the seabed at over 400°C. Explorers trek to the tops of mountains many kilometres high, and into deep caves thousands of metres underground. Rainforests are drenched by torrential rain every day, while deserts remain dry for years on end. The Earth also regularly explodes, rumbles, roars and shakes with wild weather, giant waves, earthquakes and volcanoes.

Climbing high

2 **The Earth is covered with a thick layer of rock, or 'crust'.** In some places, sections of crust have squeezed together, forcing their way upwards to make mountains. Mountains often form in a long line or group, called a mountain range. High up, it is cold and windy. This means that the tops of mountains are very icy, snowy and stormy.

Mount Everest
8850 metres
(Asia)

Mount Kilimanjaro
5895 metres
(Africa)

Mount Cook 3754 metres (Oceania)

3 **Mount Everest is the world's highest mountain.** It's on the border between Nepal and China, in the Himalayas mountain range. It is about 8850 metres high. The first people to climb to the top of Everest were Edmund Hillary and Tenzing Norgay, on May 29, 1953.

4 **The highest mountain on Earth isn't the hardest to climb.** Another peak, K2, is much tougher for mountaineers. At 8611 metres, it's the world's second-highest mountain. Its steep slopes and swirling storms make it incredibly dangerous. Fewer than 300 people have ever climbed it, and over 65 have died in the attempt.

▲ Edmund Hillary (left) and Tenzing Norgay, photographed in 1953, the year they became the first to climb Mount Everest. Hillary died in 2008.

▶ Mount Everest is so high that climbers have to climb it over several days, stopping at camps along the way.

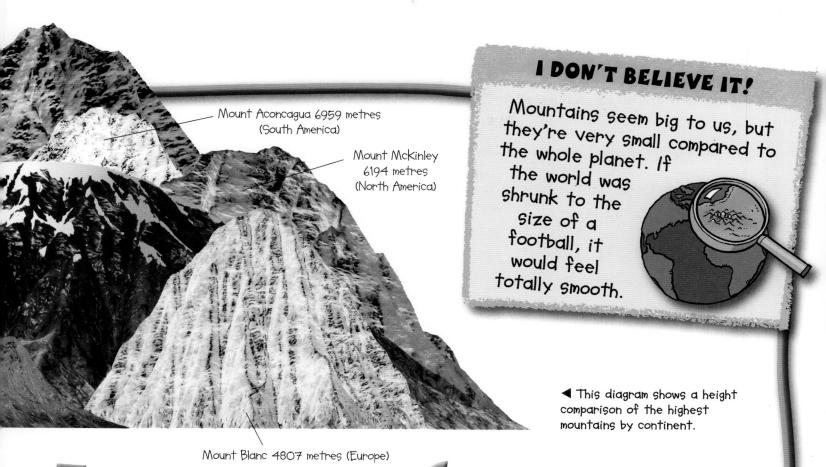

Mount Aconcagua 6959 metres
(South America)

Mount McKinley
6194 metres
(North America)

Mount Blanc 4807 metres (Europe)

◀ This diagram shows a height
comparison of the highest
mountains by continent.

5 **Most mountains are shaped like big humps — but a cliff is a sheer drop.** The east face of Great Trango, a mountain in Pakistan, is 1340 metres high, making it the tallest vertical cliff in the world. There's another giant cliff on Mount Thor in Canada, with a drop of 1250 metres. If a pebble fell off one of these cliffs, it would take more than 15 seconds to reach the bottom!

6 **Some people don't just climb to the tops of high mountains — they live there!** The town of Wenzhuan in Tibet, China, is the highest in the world. It is in the Himalayas, 5100 metres up – that's over 5 kilometres above sea level! The highest capital city is La Paz, in the Andes in Bolivia, South America. It has an altitude (height) of around 3600 metres.

▶ There are three types of mountain – volcanic, fold and block.

1. Volcanic mountains form when hot, liquid rock (lava) erupts through the Earth's crust. As the lava cools, it forms a rocky layer. With each new eruption, another layer is added.

2. Fold mountains occur when sections of the Earth's crust push against each other, making the land buckle and fold upward.

3. Block mountains occur when sections of the crust split and crack, forming faults where some sections are pushed up higher than others.

Violent volcanoes

7 A volcano is a place where hot, liquid rock (magma) bursts out of the Earth. At the Earth's surface, magma is called lava. Red-hot lava can be seen flowing or shooting out of a volcano. After a volcano erupts, the lava cools into solid rock. These rocky layers build the volcano higher and higher with each eruption.

► In 1980, a massive cloud of lava dust, ash and hot gas burst out of Mount St Helens in Washington State, USA.

8 The biggest eruptions happen when pressure builds up underground. The magma pushes up and up, but the crust on top stops it from escaping. The ground bulges and swells, until at last the magma bursts out in a huge explosion. This happened at Mount St Helens in Washington State, USA in 1980. The explosion was so huge, it blew away half the mountain!

Ash cloud

Flowing lava

Magma chamber

▲ An erupting volcano can release clouds of ash and gas as well as liquid lava.

9 The biggest volcanic eruption ever recorded was the eruption of Mount Tambora in Indonesia in 1815. The eruption was heard on the island of Sumatra, over 2000 kilometres away. Ash from the eruption filled the sky and blocked out sunlight all around the Earth. It made the weather very cold, and people called 1816 'the year without a summer'.

▲ The island of Surtsey today, more than 40 years after it appeared out of the sea.

10 Volcanoes can be killers. Victims can be burned by hot lava, hit by flying rocks, suffocated under hot ash or poisoned by gas. After the eruption, ash can mix with rainwater to make fast-flowing mud that can drown whole towns. People are in danger from eruptions because there are many towns and farms close to volcanoes. This is partly because volcanic ash helps to make the land fertile for growing crops.

11 A volcano can build a brand-new island! In 1963, smoke and steam began to billow out of the sea near Iceland. A volcano was erupting on the seabed. As the lava and ash piled up, it built a new island. The island was named Surtsey. Gradually, moss, grass and trees began to grow, and birds and insects began to live there.

VINEGAR VOLCANO MODEL

You will need:
Vinegar   Bicarbonate of soda   Red food colouring
Sand   Tray   Jug   Plastic bottle

Put a tablespoon of bicarbonate of soda in the plastic bottle. Stand the bottle on a tray and make a cone of sand around it. Put a few drops of red food colouring in half a cup of vinegar. Tip the vinegar into a jug then pour it into the bottle. In a few moments the volcano should erupt with red, frothy 'lava'.

Hot springs and fountains

12 There are natural hot baths and showers all over the world. You might think water outdoors is cold, but in some places, water meets hot rock under the ground and gets heated up. It sometimes even boils. The hot water can then make a lake or spring — or even shoot out of the ground like a fountain, forming a geyser.

▼ A mudpot, like this one in Myvatn Geothermal Area in Iceland, is a pool of hot, bubbling mud. Some mudpots are boiling hot. Others bubble as hot gases burst up through them.

Very hot water mixes with mud at the surface

▲ A mudpot forms when hot water from underground mixes with clay at the surface to make hot mud.

Steam

Very hot water

▲ Sometimes, hot underground water forms steam, which escapes through a hole or crack in the ground. These are called steam vents, or fumaroles.

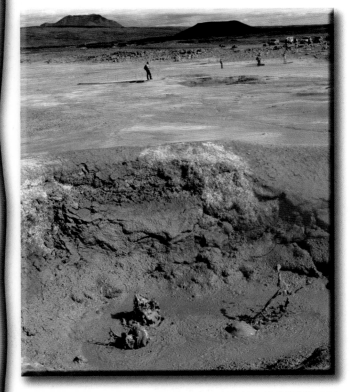

13 You shouldn't stand too close to a geyser — even if nothing's happening! A geyser is a hole in the ground that suddenly shoots out hot water and steam. Under the hole there is a water-filled chamber. Hot rock beneath it heats the water until it rises back to the surface and erupts in a giant jet of water and steam.

14 Old Faithful is one of the world's most famous geysers. Found in Yellowstone National Park USA, it gets its name because it erupts on average once every 94 minutes. Its jet of steam and water can reach 55 metres high – as high as a 15-storey building.

15 Soap helps geysers to erupt. People discovered this when they tried to use hot water pools and geysers to wash their clothes in. Soap disturbs the cold water in the chamber, helping the hot water to burst through.

▶ Strokkur (Icelandic for 'churn') is a geyser in Iceland. It erupts regularly, every 5–10 minutes, and can shoot water up to 25 metres in the air.

16 Besides geysers, the Earth's hot water can form amazing thermal (hot) springs and pools. They often occur in places where there are lots of volcanoes, such as New Zealand and Japan. Some thermal pools are famous for their beautiful colours. These are caused by millions of bacteria (tiny living things) that live in the very hot water.

▼ When rainwater seeps into the earth, it can be heated by hot rocks underground before rising back up to the surface as hot springs, pools and geysers.

Rainfall adds to groundwater

Geyser

Hot spring

Cold water travels down

Water is heated by hot rocks

Heated water starts to move upwards

Heat from Earth's interior

Rivers and waterfalls

17 The Earth is laced with thousands of rivers. Rivers are channels of water that flow towards the sea. They allow the rain that falls on the land to drain away. Rivers also provide people and animals with drinking water and a place to wash, swim and fish. A waterfall is a place where a river flows over a rocky ledge and pours down to a lower level.

18 The world's longest river is the Nile, in Africa. It starts in the area near Lake Victoria and flows north to Egypt, where it opens into the Mediterranean Sea. The journey covers nearly 6700 kilometres, and about 3470 cubic metres of water flows out of the Nile every second. The Nile provides water, a transport route, and fishing for millions of people. If it wasn't for the Nile, the civilization of ancient Egypt could not have existed.

19 Although the Nile is the longest river, the Amazon is the biggest. The Amazon flows from west to east across South America, and empties into the Atlantic Ocean. It carries 58 times as much water as the Nile, and about 200,000 cubic metres flow out of it each second. In some places, the Amazon is an amazing 60 kilometres wide.

◄ This aerial photo of the River Amazon shows how it twists and loops as it flows through the Amazon rainforest in South America.

▶ At Angel Falls, the world's highest waterfall, the water spreads out into a misty spray as it plunges down the cliff.

◀ Part of the Grand Canyon, with the Colorado River visible at the bottom of a deep gorge.

20 Angel Falls in Venezuela is the world's highest waterfall, spilling over a drop 979 metres high. It flows off the side of a very high, flat-topped mountain. Although it's the world's highest waterfall, it's not the biggest. Many waterfalls are much wider and carry more water – including Niagara Falls in North America and Victoria Falls in Africa.

21 Rivers can cut through solid rock. Over thousands of years, as a river flows, it wears away the rock around it. If the stone is quite soft, the river can carve a deep, steep-sided valley, or gorge. The Grand Canyon in Arizona, USA, is a massive gorge cut by the Colorado River. It is about 450 kilometres long, and in areas it is up to 29 kilometres wide and 1.8 kilometres deep.

Hard rock overhang

Fallen rocks

Plunge pool

Soft rock gets worn away

◀ A waterfall forms where a river flows from hard rock onto softer rock. The softer rock is worn away faster, while the overhanging ledge of hard rock gradually crumbles away. Over time, the waterfall retreats, or moves upstream.

Record-breaking lakes

22 The Caspian Sea in central Asia is actually the world's biggest lake! It covers 378,000 square kilometres. It isn't connected to true seas and oceans, but because it's so big, and is salty like the sea, some experts say it isn't a proper lake, either. The world's biggest freshwater (non-salty) lake is Lake Superior, in the USA and Canada.

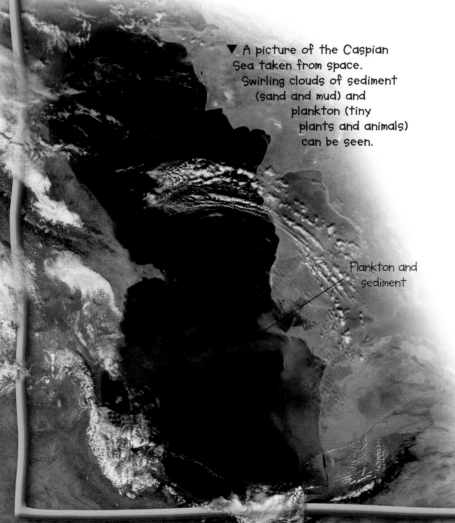

▼ A picture of the Caspian Sea taken from space. Swirling clouds of sediment (sand and mud) and plankton (tiny plants and animals) can be seen.

Plankton and sediment

23 The Dead Sea in Israel is another lake that is referred to as a sea. At 400 metres below sea level, it is the lowest lake in the world. The Dead Sea is very salty because no rivers flow out of it. All the salts and minerals that are washed into it remain there as the water evaporates in the Sun's heat. In fact the Dead Sea is nine times saltier than the real sea. It gets its name because no fish or other animals can live in such salty water.

24 The world's deepest lake is Lake Baikal in Russia. At its deepest point, it's 1700 metres deep. Because of this, it contains far more water than any other lake in the world. Twenty percent of all the unfrozen freshwater on Earth is in Lake Baikal.

QUIZ

1. Which is the biggest freshwater lake?
2. Which is the deepest lake?
3. Which is the saltiest lake?
4. In which lake might a monster live?

Answers:
1. Lake Superior 2. Lake Baikal 3. The Dead Sea 4. Loch Ness

▲ The high levels of salt in the Dead Sea mean that people can float easily in the water.

25 **The largest body of freshwater is found in North America.** On the border between the United States and Canada are the Great Lakes. They contain one-fifth of the world's freshwater – a staggering 22.8 quadrillion litres!

26 **Many lakes around the world are believed to be home to mysterious monsters.** According to legend, a monster that looks similar to a plesiosaur lives in Loch Ness in Scotland, UK. Plesiosaurs were prehistoric water reptiles that lived at the same time as the dinosaurs. Scientists think they became extinct (died out) 65 million years ago. However some people believe they may still live in Loch Ness.

◄ The five Great Lakes are situated in the USA and Canada. The biggest is Lake Superior, followed by Huron, Michigan, Erie and Ontario.

Going underground

27 Humans have climbed the world's highest mountains – but many underground caves are still unexplored. Caves are usually formed by water flowing through cracks underground. The water slowly dissolves certain types of rock, such as limestone. Over thousands of years, it can hollow out deep shafts, tunnels and even huge underground chambers.

▼ A view inside the Sarawak Chamber in Malaysia, the biggest cave chamber in the world.

28 A cave in Malaysia contains the world's biggest single underground chamber. The Sarawak chamber measures 600 metres long, 400 metres wide and at least 80 metres high. You could line up eight Boeing 747 aircraft, nose to tail, along its length – and still have space to spare.

▼ Cavers explore one of the many interconnected passageways in Mammoth Cave in Kentucky, USA.

29 The world's longest cave system is Mammoth Cave in Kentucky, USA. It has at least 570 kilometres of passageways – but explorers keep discovering more. Some experts think that only a small part of the whole cave has been explored.

▼ Caves form over thousands of years as water flows through cracks in underground rocks.

1. Rainwater seeps into cracks in rocks

2. Water dissolves rock, forming channels

3. Over time, large cave systems develop

30 In 2005, cave explorers broke a record, travelling more than 2 kilometres below the Earth's surface. They were exploring the Voronya Cave in Georgia, near Russia. It is the deepest cave in the world, with a maximum depth of 2140 metres.

31 Workers in a mine in Mexico discovered an amazing cave by accident in 2000. They were drilling a tunnel when they found a large chamber filled with enormous crystals. The crystals are made of the mineral gypsum. They look like giant swords, measuring 2 metres wide by up to 11 metres long. The chamber, which is around 300 metres deep, is now known as the Cave of Crystals.

▶ A geologist (a scientist who studies the Earth and its rocks) stands inside the amazing Cave of Crystals in Mexico.

I DON'T BELIEVE IT!

The cave salamander of central Europe is a type of amphibian. It spends its entire life in dark caves and its eyes have become blind as a result.

Extreme earthquakes

32 An earthquake happens when the Earth's crust moves suddenly. The crust trembles, cracks, or lurches up and down. Earthquakes can be disastrous. They make houses fall down, tear roads apart and destroy bridges. They can also cause tsunamis.

Fault line

Focus

Shock waves

► Earthquakes often happen when two tectonic plates slip and grind against each other. The focus is the point where the plates suddenly move.

33 Earthquakes happen because the Earth's crust is like a jigsaw. It is made up of several huge pieces called tectonic plates. The plates fit together quite neatly, covering the Earth. However they can squeeze and push against each other. Sometimes, this pushing makes the plates slip and move suddenly, causing an earthquake.

▼ Earthquakes waves travel through and across the ground in four different ways.

1. Primary waves stretch then squeeze the ground

2. Secondary waves shake the ground from side to side

3. Raleigh waves move in ripples up and down across the surface

4. Love waves travel across the surface moving the ground from side to side

▲ The San Andreas fault in California USA is a crack in the Earth's crust where two tectonic plates join. It has been the scene of several major earthquakes.

▶ Damage caused by an earthquake in Kobe, Japan, 1995. It measured 7.2 on the Richter Scale and killed more than 6000 people.

34 **Earthquakes can flatten whole cities and kill thousands.** One of the deadliest earthquakes ever hit the city of Tangshan, China in 1976. Most of the city's buildings were destroyed, and at least 240,000 people died. In 2003, an earthquake destroyed the ancient city of Bam in Iran. Over 70 percent of its buildings fell down and around 30,000 people were killed.

I DON'T BELIEVE IT!

Since ancient times, people have noticed animals behaving strangely just before earthquakes. Dogs and cats can get agitated, and herds of cattle have been known to run away.

35 **Scientists measure earthquakes using the Richter scale.** It records the amount of energy that an earthquake releases. The biggest quakes are not always the most dangerous — it depends where they happen. In a big city, a quake measuring 4 or 5 on the scale could do more damage than a quake measuring 8 or 9 in the countryside.

▼ As there are a lot of earthquakes in Japan, school children regularly practise what to do if an earthquake strikes.

36 **There are things you can do to stay safer during an earthquake.** For example, if you are outside, you should keep away from buildings and power lines. If you are indoors, you should shelter under a strong table. Some places also have quake-proof buildings.

Terrifying tsunamis

37 **A tsunami is a giant wave, or series of waves.** Tsunamis form when a large amount of water in a sea or lake is moved suddenly. This sets up a circular wave, a bit like the ripples you see when you throw a pebble into a pond. The wave then zooms outwards until it hits land.

▶ A tsunami begins as fast-travelling waves far out at sea. As they approach land, the waves slow down, but become much taller.

As the tall tsunami reaches shallow water, it surges forward onto the shore

38 **When a tsunami hits, it can smash the coast to smithereens.** Out in the ocean, tsunami waves are very long, low and fast-moving. However as a tsunami moves into shallow water, the wave slows down. All the water in it piles up, forming a powerful wall of water, often between 10 and 30 metres high. As it crashes onto the shore, it can flood towns, tear up trees and sweep away cars, buildings and people.

▼ A tsunami wave crashes onto the promenade on Ao Nang Beach, Thailand in 2004. The power and speed of a tsunami can easily sweep away cars and even entire buildings.

Decreasing depth slows speed but increases wave height

Upward wave

An earthquake beneath the sea floor causes a sudden movement of a massive column of water

40 **The tallest tsunami was higher than a skyscraper.** It occurred at Lituya Bay, in Alaska, USA, in 1958. An earthquake triggered a landslide, and rock and soil plunged into the sea. A giant tsunami, over 500 metres high, zoomed down the bay. Luckily, there were no towns there, but the wave stripped the coast of trees. A giant tsunami such as this is sometimes called a mega tsunami.

39 **Most tsunamis are caused by earthquakes under the sea.** A section of seabed shifts suddenly and the water above it is jolted upwards. Tsunamis can also happen when a landslide or volcanic eruption throws a large amount of rock into the sea, pushing the water aside. This happened when Krakatau, a volcano in Indonesia, erupted in 1883. The tsunamis it caused killed 36,000 people.

41 **A tsunami in the Indian Ocean in 2004 was the deadliest ever recorded.** It was caused by a huge undersea earthquake near the coast of Indonesia. Tsunami waves spread across the ocean and swamped coasts in Indonesia, Thailand, Sri Lanka, India and the Maldive Islands. Around 230,000 people were killed.

▼ The town of Kalutara in Sri Lanka, shown in satellite images before (left) and after (right) being swamped by the deadly 2004 tsunami.

42 Deserts occur in places where it's hard for rain to reach. Most rain comes from clouds that form over the sea and blow onto the land. If there's a big mountain range, the clouds never reach the other side. An area called a rainshadow desert forms. Deserts also form in the middle of continents. The land there is so far from the sea, rainclouds rarely reach it.

▲ The Namib Desert in the southwest of Africa contains some of the biggest sand dunes in the world.

QUIZ

Which of these things would be useful if you were lost in the desert?

1. Mirror
2. Woolly blanket
3. Swimming costume
4. Umbrella

Answers:
1, 2 and 4.
You should not wear swimming gear in case of sunburn.

43 The world's biggest desert used to be a swamp! The Sahara Desert takes up most of northern Africa. It is made up of 9 million square kilometres of dry sand, pebbles and boulders. There are some oases too, where freshwater springs flow out of the ground. Animal bones and objects left by ancient peoples show that around 6000 years ago, the Sahara Desert was green and swampy. Lots of hippos, crocodiles and humans lived there.

▼ These sand piles show the relative sizes of the world's biggest deserts.

Sahara Desert
9,269,000 km²

Australian Desert
3,800,000 km²

Arabian Desert
1,300,000 km²

Gobi Desert
1,040,000 km²

Kalahari Desert
520,000 km²

44 Deserts aren't always hot.

The hottest temperature ever recorded was 57.8°C in Libya. However deserts can be cold, too. The average temperature in the Atacama Desert, South America is only about 10°C. In the Gobi Desert in Asia, winter temperatures can drop to −40°C. All deserts can be cold at night, as there are no clouds to stop heat escaping.

▲ Desert roses aren't plants. They occur when desert minerals, such as gypsum, combine with sand to form crystals.

▶ Sand dunes form in different shapes and patterns, depending on the type of wind and sand in the desert. The blue arrows indicate the wind direction.

Barchan dune

Parabolic dune

Star dune

Seif dune

Transverse dune

45 The world's driest desert is the Aatacama Desert in Chile, South America.

This desert is right next to the sea! It formed because in South America, rainclouds blow from east to west. They drop their rain on the Amazon rainforest, but cannot get past the Andes mountains. On the other side of the Andes, next to the Pacific Ocean, is the Atacama Desert. It is so dry that people who died there 9000 years ago have been preserved as mummies.

▶ An oasis is a freshwater spring in a desert. Oases form when water stored deep underground meets a barrier of rock that it can't soak through, and rises to the desert surface.

46 Even in dry deserts, there is water if you know where to look.

Desert plants, such as cactuses store water in their stems, leaves or spines. When rain does fall, it seeps into the ground and stays there. Desert people and animals chew desert plants or dig into the ground to find enough water.

The ends of the Earth

47 The Earth is round, but it has two 'ends' – the North Pole and the South Pole. The Earth is constantly spinning around an imaginary line called the axis. At the ends of this axis are the poles. Here, it is always cold, because the poles are so far from the Sun.

▲ The position of the poles means they receive little heat from the Sun.

48 At the North Pole, the average temperature is –20°C. At the South pole, it's much colder – about –50°C. It's hard for humans to survive in this cold. Water droplets in your breath would freeze on your face. If you were to touch something made of metal with your bare hand, it would freeze onto your skin and stick there.

49 The area around the North Pole is called the Arctic. Parts of Europe, Asia and North America reach into the Arctic, but most of it is actually the Arctic Ocean. Many animals live in the Arctic. Polar bears and seals live on the ice and Arctic foxes, Arctic hares and snowy owls live on the land. The sea around the pole is mainly frozen. Scientists have found the ice is melting because of global warming. This is happening because pollution in the air is trapping heat close to the Earth, making it warm up.

Carbon dioxide layer traps heat

Sun

Trapped heat from the Sun bounces back to Earth

◄ Pollution in the form of carbon dioxide gas traps heat from the Sun, making the Earth warm up. This is one reason that the polar ice is melting.

▲ There are several different species (types) of penguins living in Antarctica. These emperor penguins and their chicks are the largest species.

50 The Antarctic is mostly made up of a huge continent, called Antarctica. Much of it is covered in a layer of solid ice up to 4.7 kilometres thick. The Antarctic is colder than the Arctic because its thick ice and mountains make it very high, and the air is colder higher up. Because Antarctica is so big, the seas around it cannot warm it very much. Little wildlife lives here, but it is home to lots of penguins.

I DON'T BELIEVE IT!

Explorers at the poles sometimes lose body parts. If they let their fingers, toes or nose get too cold, they can get frostbite. Blood stops flowing to these parts, and they can turn black and fall off.

51 Explorers didn't make it to the poles until the 20th century. US explorer Robert Peary and his team reached the North Pole in 1909. Soon afterwards, two explorers raced to reach the South Pole. Norwegian Roald Amundsen arrived first, in December 1911. British explorer Robert Scott arrived one month later – but he and his men died on their way home.

◄ There are no towns or cities in Antarctica as it's so cold, but people do go there to explore and to study nature. They sometimes use snowmobiles to travel around on the snow and ice.

Glaciers and icebergs

52 **About two percent of the water in the world is permanently frozen as ice.** The ice is found at the chilly polar regions, and on high mountains where the air is freezing cold. On steep slopes, the ice creeps downhill, like a very slow river. This kind of ice 'river' is called a glacier. On high mountains, glaciers flow downhill until they reach warmer air and start to melt. At the poles, many glaciers flow into the sea.

▶ A glacier develops deep cracks called crevasses as it moves downhill. The lower end of a glacier is called the 'snout'.

Snout

Crevasse

53 **One of the world's biggest glaciers, not including the ice at the poles, is the Siachen Glacier in the Himalayas.** It is 78 kilometres long and, in places, its ice is over 100 metres thick. India and Pakistan have been fighting a war over who the glacier belongs to since 1984. It has been home to hundreds of soldiers for more than 20 years.

▼ Instead of melting on the way down a mountain, this glacier in Prince William Sound, Alaska is flowing into a fjord.

54 Glaciers have shaped the Earth. As a glacier flows down a mountain, the heavy ice pushes and scrapes at the soil and rocks. This carves a huge, U-shaped valley, known as a glacial valley. 20,000 years ago, when the Earth was in an Ice Age, glaciers covered much more of the land than they do now. Since then, many have melted, revealing their glacial valleys.

55 Icebergs exist because of glaciers. At the poles, glaciers flow downhill to the sea. There, the ice is slowly pushed out into the water, where it starts to float. Every so often, a large chunk of the glacier breaks off and floats away into the sea. This is an iceberg and it drifts until it melts.

56 Icebergs are a problem for ships. As an iceberg floats, only about one-tenth of it sticks up out of the sea. The rest is below the surface. Many icebergs have odd, lumpy shapes. This means that a ship can bump into the underwater part of an iceberg, even if the part above water looks far away. Icebergs have damaged and sunk many ships, including the famous ocean liner *Titanic* in 1912.

▼ These penguins are on an iceberg in the Southern Ocean, close to Antarctica. A huge mass of ice can be seen below the water's surface.

MAKE AN ICEBERG

You will need:
Plastic container   Clear bowl   Water

1. Fill the container with water and put it in the freezer.
2. When frozen, remove your 'iceberg' from the container.
3. Fill the clear bowl with water and place your iceberg in it.
4. Look through the side to see how much of your iceberg is underwater, and what shape it makes.

57 **About 70 percent of the Earth's surface is covered by ocean.** The oceans cover about 361 million square kilometres and they are all connected. The average depth of the ocean is 3750 metres. Over 90 percent of the Earth's species (types) of living things live in the oceans.

58 **The deepest point in all the world's oceans is called Challenger Deep.** It is in the Mariana Trench in the Pacific Ocean and is 10,923 metres deep – almost 11 kilometres. A tower of 3500 elephants, one of top of the next, could stand in it without touching the surface. In 1960, two explorers, Jacques Piccard and Don Walsh, visited the bottom of Challenger Deep in a diving vessel called *Trieste*.

59 **If you were sitting at the bottom of the deep ocean, you'd be squashed flat.** At great depths, the weight of all the water above presses from all sides. At the bottom of Challenger Deep, the water pressure is more than 1000 times stronger than at the surface. It's cold, too – only just above freezing point. People can only go there inside specially built diving machines with thick walls that can resist the pressure and cold.

▲ The *Trieste*, which made the deepest deep-sea dive ever in 1960, was made of a large tank full of gasoline to give buoyancy, with a small round passenger chamber fixed underneath.

Oceanic crust

Deep-sea trench

Ocean ridge

Underwater volcano

Challenger Deep

► This map shows the ridges, trenches, plains and mountains within the world's oceans, as well as those on land.

ARCTIC OCEAN

PACIFIC OCEAN

ATLANTIC OCEAN

INDIAN OCEAN

SOUTHERN OCEAN

60 One of the world's most extreme environments is found under the sea.
At hydrothermal vents, incredibly hot water bubbles out from inside the Earth at temperatures of up to 400°C. Around the hot vents live unusual creatures such as giant tubeworms and sea spiders, and tiny bacteria that feed on the minerals dissolved in the hot water. Hydrothermal vents were only discovered in 1977.

▼ A cross-section of the seabed. It usually slopes gently away from the shore, then drops steeply down to a flat plain.

61 Sea level — the height of the sea — is about the same all over the world.
It changes over time, as the Earth's temperature varies. About 20,000 years ago, during the Ice Age, the sea level was 130 metres lower than it is now. At the moment, the sea level is rising because global warming is making ice melt at the poles.

Continental shelf

Continental slope

Plain

TRUE OR FALSE?

1. Challenger Deep is deeper than Mount Everest is tall.
2. The water at the bottom of the sea is always very cold.
3. Sea creatures bigger than blue whales could exist.

Answers:
1. True — Everest is only 8850 m high. 2. False — the water can be hot around hydrothermal vents 3. True — the sea is so big, it could contain species unknown to science

Raining cats and dogs

62 **It may seem like bad weather, but we need rain.** Rain happens because the Sun's heat makes water in the sea evaporate. It turns into a gas, rises into the air and forms clouds. The clouds then blow over the land. They cool down, turn back into water, and fall as rain. If this didn't happen, there would be no life on Earth – all living things need water to survive.

▶ Heavy rain is accompanied by big, black clouds.

64 **In rainforests it rains almost every day.** Rainforests are found in the warm tropical parts of the Earth, near the Equator. The hot sunshine makes lots of water evaporate and fall as rain. A lot of the rain that falls on a rainforest never touches the ground. It collects on the treetops, then evaporates into the air, before falling as rain again.

63 **The world's rainiest place is Meghalaya, an area of north-east India.** Some towns there, such as Cherrapunji and Mawsynram, get around 11,500 millimetres of rain a year. If the rain didn't drain away or evaporate, it would be 11.5 metres deep after one year!

MAKE A RAIN GAUGE

You will need:
Jar or food container with a flat base and straight sides   Ruler   Notebook

1. Find a good place to put your container, in a shady spot, away from buildings.

2. Dig a small hole in the ground to fit it into, or put stones around it to hold it in place.

3. Each day at the same time, measure the depth of the water then empty your container.

4. Record your results in a notebook to keep

▼ Water continually rises from the sea into the air, falls on the land as rain, then flows back to the sea. This is called the water cycle.

As clouds cool down, they turn back into liquid water and fall as rain

Water evaporates from plants and the ground

Rainwater flows into rivers and back into the sea

Water evaporates from the sea and blows over the land

65 It doesn't really rain cats and dogs — but there have been reports of red rain, and showers of frogs, fish and crabs. Frogs and toads were reported falling in Minneapolis, USA in 1901. It has rained fish in Singapore, and crabs in the UK. These strange showers probably happen when tornadoes or strong winds sweep up water containing living creatures, which then fall to the ground.

▼ A rickshaw driver and passenger travel through monsoon floods in India. When rains are heavy, streets turn to rivers and people's homes may be washed away.

66 A monsoon is a very rainy season. Monsoons happen in parts of Asia, especially India, in late summer. The land gets very hot and heats the air above it. The hot air rises, and this sucks in damp, cloudy air from the sea. The clouds rush over the land. When they meet the Himalayan mountains, they rise and get colder. This creates lots of rain, especially in northern India.

67 **Lightning is a giant spark of electricity.** It happens when tiny droplets of water and ice swirl around inside a stormcloud. This makes the cloud develop a strong electrical charge. Eventually, a spark jumps between the base of the cloud and the ground. This allows electricity to flow, releasing the electrical charge. We see the spark as a flash or 'bolt' of lightning.

Positive charge

Negative charge

Negative charge from the cloud meets a positive charge from the ground to create lightning

▲ During a thunderstorm, negative electrical charge builds up at the base of a cloud, while the ground has a positive charge. A lightning spark jumps between them to release the charge.

I DON'T BELIEVE IT!

At any one time, there are around 2000 thunderstorms happening on Earth. Lightning strikes somewhere in the world about 100 times every second.

68 **Thunder and lightning go together.** In fact, thunder is the sound of lightning. When a lightning bolt jumps through the air, it is very hot. It can reach a temperature of 30,000°C. It heats the air around it very quickly. Heat makes air expand (get bigger). It expands so suddenly that it pushes against the air around it, and creates a shock wave. The wave travels through the air and our ears detect it as a loud boom.

69 Long ago, people used to think lightning was a punishment sent by their gods. However from the 1500s, scientists began learning about electricity and how it worked. Around 1750, US scientist Benjamin Franklin found that lightning was a kind of electricity. He invented the lightning conductor to protect buildings from lightning damage. It is a metal pole that can be fixed to tall buildings. If lightning strikes, the electrical charge runs down the pole and down a metal wire, then flows safely into the ground.

◄ You can clearly see the lightning conductor on the spire of this cathedral in Liverpool, UK.

70 Lightning can strike the same person twice — or more. A US park ranger named Roy Sullivan was struck by lightning seven times during his life. It is quite rare for lightning to strike people, and most of those who are struck, survive. However lightning does kill over 2000 people around the world each year.

▼ Fulgarites occur when lightning strikes sand. The high temperature makes the sand melt. It eventually cools into hollow tubes.

71 Lightning can make glass. Glass is made by heating up sand. When lightning strikes in a sandy desert or on a sandy beach, this happens naturally. At the place where the lightning hits the ground, it creates a tubelike tunnel of glass in the sand. These natural glass tubes are called fulgurites.

Hammered by hail

72 **Hail doesn't happen often — but it can be one of the scariest kinds of weather.** When it hails, balls of hard, heavy ice fall out of the sky. Hailstones are usually small, about the size of peas. However they can be bigger — marble-sized, egg-sized or even tennis-ball-sized. Sometimes they're big enough to crush crops, smash car windows or even kill people.

▼ A man shows off scars on his back — the result of being hit by hailstones while riding a bicycle.

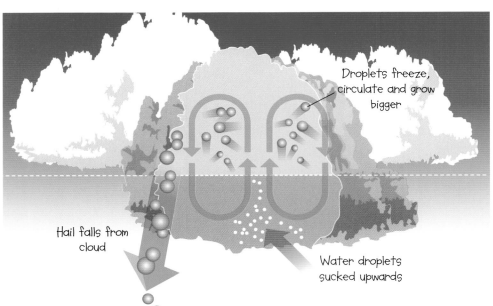

Droplets freeze, circulate and grow bigger

Hail falls from cloud

Water droplets sucked upwards

▲ Hailstones only form inside thunderclouds. Eventually they become too heavy, and fall to the ground as lumps of ice.

73 **A hailstone needs a seed.** Hailstones form inside thunderclouds when very cold water droplets freeze onto a tiny object — the 'seed'. It could be a speck of dust or a plant seed carried into the sky by the wind. The tiny hailstone is then tossed around by strong winds inside the cloud. More and more layers of ice build up around it, until it is so heavy that it falls to the ground.

74 **The biggest hailstone ever recorded was the size of a melon!** This giant hailstone fell in Aurora, Nebraska, USA in 2003. It measured 18 centimetres across. The biggest hailstones are usually 'aggregate' hailstones. They are made of smaller hailstones that have clumped together before falling to the ground.

◀ The largest hailstone on record is shown here at actual size. It fell in Nebraska, USA in 2003.

I DON'T BELIEVE IT!

Hail usually only falls for a few minutes. However a hailstorm in Kansas, USA in 1959 went on for over an hour. It covered the ground with a layer of hailstones 46 centimetres deep!

75 **Sometimes a hailstone forms around a living thing.** A farmer in Quebec, Canada reported finding a frog inside a hailstone in 1864. In 1894, a hailstone with a turtle inside was reported to have fallen on Bovina, Mississippi, USA. Smaller creatures such as spiders and flies are often trapped inside hailstones.

76 **The world's worst hailstorms happen in Northern India and Bangladesh.** Hailstones often destroy crops, and people are regularly injured and killed. In 1888, a hailstorm in India killed around 250 people and more than 1000 sheep and goats.

▶ People in Mexico City, Mexico, shovel hailstones after a huge hailstorm on 3 August, 2006.

Extreme snow and ice

77 An ice storm isn't stormy — but it is **dangerous.** Cold rain falls onto freezing cold surfaces. The rain freezes solid, forming a thick layer of ice on the ground, trees and other objects. Ice storms cause 'black ice'— invisible ice on roads that causes accidents. Ice-laden trees fall down, breaking power lines and cutting off roads.

◀ Overburdened by the weight of ice from an ice storm, this tree has collapsed across a road.

▲ An avalanche thunders downhill in Silverton, Colorado, USA. This avalanche was started deliberately by dropping explosives, in order to make the mountains safer for visitors.

78 An avalanche is a massive pile of snow crashing down a mountainside. Avalanches can happen whenever lots of snow piles up at the top of a slope. They can be deadly if the snow lands on top of mountain walkers or skiers. Sometimes, big avalanches bury whole houses or even whole villages.

79 A blizzard, or snowstorm, is even more dangerous than an ice storm. If you get caught outdoors in a blizzard, it's very easy to get lost. Falling snow fills the air, making it impossible to see. Thick snowdrifts build up, making it hard to walk or drive. People have lost their way and died in blizzards, just a short distance from safety.

▲ Ice can form beautiful crystal patterns as it freezes across a window or car windscreen.

QUIZ
Which of these things could help you survive if you were lost in the snow?

1. Woolly hat
2. Magazine
3. Chocolate
4. Torch
5. Metal camping plate

Answer:
All of them!

80 **If you get stuck in a blizzard or avalanche, a hole in the snow can keep you warm.** Snow is a great insulator. as heat does not flow through it very well. If you curl up inside a hole dug in the snow, it traps the heat from your body and keeps it close to you. Many people have survived blizzards by making snow holes.

▼ A man uses a reindeer sledge to collect remains of a woolly mammoth discovered buried in ice.

81 **We put food in a freezer to keep it fresh — and the same thing happens in nature.** Snow and ice can stop dead bodies from rotting away. Woolly mammoths that lived 10,000 years ago have been dug out of the ice in northern Russia, perfectly preserved. In 1991, the body of a 5000-year-old man was found in the ice in mountains in Austria. He was nicknamed Ötzi the Iceman.

Twisting tornadoes

82 **Tornadoes are also called twisters.** A tornado is an incredibly powerful windstorm that twists around in a swirling 'vortex' shape. It forms a narrow funnel or tube, stretching from the clouds to the ground. Tornadoes often look dark because of all the dirt, dust and broken objects that they pick up as they travel across the land.

83 **You can sometimes tell when a tornado is coming, because the sky turns green.** Tornadoes usually develop from thunderclouds. Scientists are not sure exactly how they form. They think that as warm, damp air rises, drier, colder air is pulled in and begins to swirl around it. This creates a spinning tube of wind that moves along the ground. A tornado can travel at up to 80 kilometres an hour.

84 **Tornadoes contain some of the fastest winds on the planet.** Wind inside a tornado can move at up to 500 kilometres an hour. This powerful wind can cause terrible damage. Tornadoes smash buildings, tear off roofs, make bridges collapse, and suck out doors and windows. They can pick up people, animals and cars, and carry them through the air. In 2006, a tornado in Missouri, USA picked up 19-year-old Matt Suter and carried him nearly 400 metres. He survived with only cuts and bruises.

Cold front

Warm front

◀ Tornadoes often form where a front, or mass, of cold air meets warm air. They spin around each other and form a funnel shape.

TORNADO IN A BOTTLE

You will need:
Two plastic drinks bottles the same size
Water   Sticky tape

1. Fill one of the bottles almost full with water.

2. Position the second bottle upside-down on top of the first, so that their necks join together. Tape them together firmly.

3. Turn both bottles over and swirl them around in a circle as fast as you can.

4. When you hold them still, you should see a tornado shape as the water forms a vortex.

◄ A large, terrifying tornado snakes down to the ground from the base of a big thundercloud.

85 Damaging tornadoes happen most often in Tornado Alley. This is an area which stretches across the middle of the USA, between the states of Texas and Illinois. Tornadoes are most common there in the tornado season, from April to August. The Great Tri-State Tornado of 1925 was one of the worst ever. It roared through Missouri, Illionois and Indiana, travelling 350 kilometres. It destroyed 15,000 homes and killed 695 people.

◄ The shaded area on this map shows the part of the USA known as Tornado Alley, where tornadoes are most common.

86 Sometimes, tornadoes occur in deserts, or over the sea. In sandy deserts, small tornadoes pick up sand and carry it along in a whirling tower. They are called sand devils or dust devils. Tornadoes over the sea can suck up water in the same way, and carry it for long distances. They are known as waterspouts.

Minneapolis
Sioux Falls
Chicago
Denver
Kansas City
St. Louis
Wichita
USA
Amarilo
Oklahoma City
Dallas
New Orleans
Houston

MEXICO

Howling hurricanes

▶ A man struggles through the high winds of Hurricane Andrew that hit the USA in 1992. Only Hurricane Katrina in 2005 has been more destructive.

87 **A hurricane is a huge, swirling mass of stormclouds.** Hurricanes form over the ocean, but often travel onto land where they cause floods and destroy whole towns. A typical hurricane is about 500 kilometres wide. In the middle is a small, circular area with no clouds in it, about 70 kilometres wide. This is called the 'eye' of the hurricane.

88 **Hurricanes begin in the tropics where the ocean is warm.** The ocean surface has to be about 27°C or warmer for a hurricane to start. Warm, wet air rises, forming rainclouds. These begin to swirl in a spiral, caused by the spinning Earth. If the winds reach 118 kilometres an hour, the storm is called a hurricane. Hurricane winds can be as fast as 240 kilometres an hour.

89 **Hurricanes have names!** Each year, all hurricanes are given names from a list. There are six lists altogether, so the same names are repeated every six years. If a hurricane becomes famous – like Hurricane Katrina in 2005 – the list is changed so that name does not reappear.

I DON'T BELIEVE IT!

At the 'eye' of a hurricane, in the middle of the storm, it's calm and quiet, not stormy at all. The eye only lasts a short time, until the rest of the storm arrives.

90 The word 'hurricane' is only used to describe storms in the Atlantic Ocean. The scientific name for this type of storm is a tropical cyclone. The same type of storm in the Indian Ocean is known as a cyclone, and in the Pacific Ocean it is called a typhoon.

▲ A satellite view from space showing a hurricane swirling across the Gulf of Mexico.

91 Hurricanes and other tropical cyclones can cause terrible disasters. When Hurricane Katrina struck the southern coast of the USA in August 2005, it damaged many cities on the coasts of Mississippi and Louisiana. In New Orleans, huge waves broke through the flood barriers and more than 80 percent of the city was flooded. The hurricane killed over 1800 people and caused damage costing over $80 billion. The Bhola cyclone, which hit Bangladesh in 1970, killed over 300,000 people.

92 Scientists think hurricanes are getting worse. Global warming means that the Earth's temperature is rising, so the seas are getting warmer. This means that more hurricanes are likely. Hurricanes are also becoming bigger and more powerful, as there is more heat energy to fuel them.

▼ These buildings near Lake Pontchartrain, Louisiana, USA, were destroyed by Hurricane Katrina in 2005.

Water, water everywhere

93 **A flood happens when water overflows and covers what is normally land.** Floods can be caused by rivers overflowing their banks after heavy rain. The sea can also flood the land with large waves or tsunamis. Floods can be useful – some rivers flood every year in the rainy season, bringing water and mud that make farmland moist and fertile. However most floods are bad news.

▲ A satellite image of the River Nile in Egypt flowing into the Mediterranean Sea. The green triangular area is the Nile Delta. The Nile used to flood each summer, spreading fertile silt across the land. These floods are now controlled by the Aswan Dam in southern Egypt.

▼ A woman carries a precious pot of clean drinking water through dirty floodwaters during a flood in Bangladesh in 1998.

94 Floods can cause death and destruction. When floodwater flows into houses, it fills them with mud, rubbish and sewage (smelly waste from drains and toilets). It ruins electrical appliances, carpets and furniture. After a flood, homes have to be completely cleaned out and repaired – costing huge amounts of money. Even worse, fast-flowing floodwater can sweep away people, cars and even buildings.

95 Floods often cause water shortages. Although there's water everywhere, it's dirty and not safe to drink. The dirty water can fill up water supply pipes and water treatment works. They can't supply clean water, and the taps have to be switched off. During bad floods, the emergency services have to deliver water in bottles or tanks, so that people have enough clean water to drink.

▲ Heavy floods hit many parts of England in the summer of 2007. This aerial photo shows Tewkesbury in Gloucestershire.

96 More floods are coming. Because of global warming, the Earth is heating up. In some areas, this means more water will evaporate into the air, causing more clouds and more rain. Global warming also means higher sea levels, so more areas of land are at risk of being flooded.

I DON'T BELIEVE IT!

The Bible tells of a great flood that covered the world in water. Some scientists think flood stories may be based on flooding that happened around 10,000 years ago, as sea levels rose when ice melted after the last Ice Age.

▼ This car was caught in a flash flood (a sudden, unexpected flood) in Texas, USA. Flash floods can wash entire towns away.

45

Disastrous droughts

97 A drought is a shortage of rainfall that leaves the land dry. Deserts hardly ever get rain, and are dry and dusty all the time. A drought happens when a place gets much less rain than usual. Scientists don't always know why weather patterns change. However, this can be caused by changes in the oceans. Every few years, a change in sea temperatures in the Pacific, called El Niño, affects weather around the world and causes droughts.

▲ During drought conditions, water is precious. Without it people, animals and plants will die.

Equator

SOUTH AMERICA

Warm water

PACIFIC OCEAN

AUSTRALIA

Cold water

▲ El Niño is a warming of surface ocean waters in the eastern Pacific that can lead to flooding and drought around the world.

98 Droughts are disastrous for people, animals and plants. A shortage of rain means crops can't grow properly, and herds of animals can't get enough drinking water. So people face food and water shortages. Dried-out grass and trees can easily catch fire, and loose dust can blow up into blinding dust storms. Droughts can also cause wars, when people are forced to leave their lands and flock into other areas.

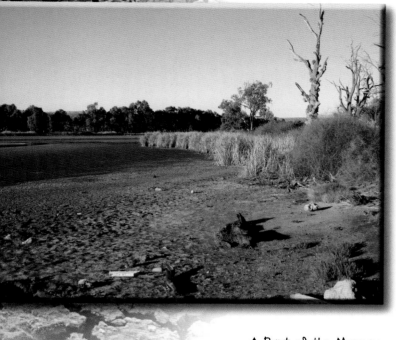

99

Droughts have always happened. They are mentioned in many ancient books, such as the Bible and the writings of the ancient Mesopotamians, who lived in the area around what is now Iraq. However, scientists think that today, global warming is making some droughts worse. As the world gets warmer, weather patterns are changing. Some areas, such as eastern Australia, are now having worse droughts than they used to.

▲ Part of the Murray River in southern Australia, usually flowing with water, lies empty during a drought.

100

The 'Dust Bowl' was a great drought disaster that hit the USA in the 1930s. Several years of drought dried out farm soil in the central states of the USA, such as Oklahoma and Kansas. It blew away in huge dust storms, and farmers could not grow their crops. Hundreds of thousands of people had to leave the area. Many trekked west in search of new lives and jobs.

TRUE OR FALSE?

1. Droughts make forest fires more likely.
2. The Dust Bowl is a volcano in the USA.
3. El Niño is a temperature change in the Indian Ocean.

Answers:
1. True. Droughts make forests drier so they burn more easily 2. False. The Dust Bowl was a drought 3. False. El Niño is in the Pacific Ocean

◀ A massive dust storm about to engulf a farm during the Dust Bowl years. Caused by drought conditions, these storms devastated the American prairies.

Index

Entries in **bold** refer to main subject entries. Entries in *italics* refer to illustrations.